Epiphanies

of a Middle-Aged Princess

Epiphanies

of a Middle-Aged Princess

Kathy Oakes

iUniverse, Inc.

New York Bloomington Shanghai

Epiphanies of a Middle-Aged Princess

iUniverse books may be ordered through booksellers or by contacting:

iUniverse
1663 Liberty Drive
Bloomington, IN 47403
www.iuniverse.com
1-800-Authors (1-800-288-4677)

Because of the dynamic nature of the Internet, any Web addresses or links contained in this book may have changed since publication and may no longer be valid.

The views expressed in this work are solely those of the author and do not necessarily reflect the views of the publisher, and the publisher hereby disclaims any responsibility for them.

ISBN: 978-0-595-48125-5 (pbk)
ISBN: 978-0-595-60223-0 (ebk)

Printed in the United States of America

To Bethany, Allyson, Kara, and Jeffrey.
You have given me more glimpses of God than anyone on this earth.
I pray you will learn from my mistakes and
enjoy discovering epiphanies of your own.

Contents

Epiphanies Happen

Have you ever noticed that we can be perking along, minding our own business in the humdrum of our ordinary lives, and then it happens—an epiphany! Sometimes they get our attention with a shout, sometimes with a whisper, but they always provide clear guidance if we listen.

Recently one of these hit me; my husband, whom I love dearly, and I are *one*. We have been married for twenty years, so this is not a completely new revelation, but it is, nonetheless, weighty. We are *one*. I find myself astounded each time I explore that thought. *WE* are one.

When we were young, little dreamers, we often ended our dates at a peaceful lake where we sat on a lovely bench that looked out over the possibilities of a lifetime. We would watch the sun go down and dream out loud of our future. I often relive those wonderful conversations in my head and think back on who we were back in the beginning. Taking this kind of mental inventory of the wonders of the past keeps me grounded as I continually move into the future.

Not too long ago, my husband and I were lying in bed, just talking about life. The conversation reminded me of our lake talks but without the bench or the sunset. We talked about the next season of our lives and where we wanted to go, what we wanted to accomplish, and so on. It was then that the epiphany hit me. In the last twenty years, as one we have accomplished all of the things on his dream to-do list, but we have yet to even get started on mine.

Now don't get me wrong; it is not like I have done nothing but sit around and eat bonbons for two decades. It is just that God has redirected my goals, and even desires, and that has been a good thing. Despite that fact, I felt the need to consider my epiphany in greater detail.

A few nights later, we climbed into bed and began our nightly chatter.

"Jeff, whose life are we leading here?" I asked.

"Ours, honey," he responded, "We are leading our life."

"Hmmm. Well, while I agree with you one hundred percent, honey, being a woman, I have two hundred percent of opinion to weigh in with. So flow with me here as we investigate this a little further," I warned.

He looked worried, but he agreed.

"If I died, would your life or life habits change at all?" Now he really looked worried and tried to comfort me by touching my arm and giving me that worried plea that husbands give, "now honey ..." but I interrupted.

"No, seriously, honey. If I died, would your life or life habits change?"

He opened his mouth as if to speak but stopped short, understanding that I had not yet passed the permission-to-speak wand to him. Instead I began to answer for him. He is a wise man and knows that sometimes keeping quiet is best, so he indulged me a little longer.

"No, your life would not!" I decreed. "You would eat at the same restaurants, you would live in the same house, you would drive the same car, and go to the same places, and you would shop at the same stores. You are living your life!"

"If you died, however," I continued, lowering my brow and my voice as a warning that he had better listen closely, "I would never eat buckets of chips and salsa again. I would sell this house and move into something newer on one level. I would still go to the same church, hang out with the same people, and probably even drive the same car (maybe), but I would not shop where you like to shop, I would buy more gourmet cheeses at the deli, and I repeat, I would not eat anything that smelled like jalapeños ever again."

At that point, his worried expression gave way to raucous laughter as he wrapped me up in one of his comforting bear hugs. I am glad my epiphany provided him with such quality entertainment.

This epiphany started me on a path of discovery, as they often do. It made me aware that the little revelations I get are actually divine traffic lights. Sometimes they direct me and sometimes they shake me, but each one is an *encounter with God's truth.*

If life is a journey, how do we find our way down the winding roads and through the muddled intersections? How do we know when to stop and when to go? Epiphanies are signposts that take us in the right direction.

Every woman has her own journey to make, and, while no two paths are alike, every path shares the same map. We must learn to close our eyes and trust ourselves, remember that pit stops are OK as long as we don't stay too long, understand that detours happen and that fuel is necessary, remember to always keep our identification and our minds with us at all times, take pictures along the way, and, most importantly, stay the course.

This book should serve to remind us of all of those things. The stories here should be taken in as you wish, as one leisurely afternoon meal or sampled in small bites over several weeks. This book should most definitely to be shared with friends, because like the good in our lives, a fun book should never be kept a secret. Now there is an important little epiphany.

1

PIT STOPS

"My first love, you're every breath that I take. You're every step I make," or something along those lines. You know the song, right? "Endless Love."

How can we travel without making pit stops along the way? Discovering love has got to be one of the most complexly simple "potty breaks" we take in life.

I compare falling in love for the first time to a potty break because the phrase represents the urgency we feel. When it hits us, it hits us, and, well, we just have to stop. I know women who have stopped and stayed. I was one who stopped, let nature run its course, and then got back on the journey.

I think I was in the eighth grade when Paul, a tenth-grader, handed me a note as I got on the school bus to go home. I did not really know him. I knew he played football, and he seemed very mature. I do not remember what the note said. It did not matter what the note said. What mattered is what was communicated. Somehow I knew that I was the most beautiful person he had ever laid eyes on and that he could not live if he did not sit by me at lunchtime the next day.

Being a very considerate young lady, I of course made lunch plans at his table the next day. Somehow, a friendship developed over what became daily lunches together. The next year I was finally a freshman, and he wanted to take me on a date. An unchaperoned car date, thank you very much. This was big stuff. Uncharted territory.

My parents agreed to let him bring me home from eating pizza after the first football game of the season. I was so nervous. I was so excited. I do not know who won the game that night. The only thing on my mind was wishing the game could end.

My parents drove me to the Pizza Hut where an enormous number of our high school friends had gathered to celebrate or commiserate; it did not matter to me. I did not feel young that night. I went from booth to booth chatting with everyone like Scarlet O'Hara at a picnic. Pizza, football, the smell of fall; it was perfect. That night held all the ingredients for love.

Finally, the inevitable moment came. Paul would drive me home. We stood at the door waving good-bye to all of our friends. It was as if we all shared a secret; we all laughed.

He opened the door of his father's slick Impala for me. Where should I sit? Closer? Would that send the wrong message? Close to the door? What would that say? I wished I had thought this through beforehand. I could have discussed it with my mother. I would have discussed it with my friends. There was to be a depression on the passenger side, so that seemed like a safe spot.

When he got into the car, he was painfully quiet. He whistled quietly to a song on the radio. I thought it was funny to watch his Adam's apple dance. He was gawky and awkward and cute, all at once. He took little pauses from whistling, until at last the pause became permanent. As I turned to look at him, ready to break the silence, I noticed he looked a little pale. I could tell he was swallowing hard.

Then it happened. To this day my friends do not believe me, but it really did happen. He puked everywhere.

He managed to get the car onto the side of road where he practically fell out the door to finish heaving. As soon as that car had slowed down to ten miles per hour I jumped too. I fell out onto the side of the road where I laughed uncontrollably. Call me a woman of compassion, but I thought it was hilarious.

The poor thing asked me for the box of tissues under the seat. But I wisely refused to get back into the car until he cleaned up his mess and had rolled down all the windows. He got sick twice more on the way home.

The normal questions floated through my head that night. Would he try to kiss me? Would he not? If he tries, what should I do? But as he walked me to the door, I had no fear. There was no question in my mind. I did not have to worry. I stepped up onto the porch so that I could look him in the eyes, and I said, "Don't even think I'm kissing you good night!"

I ran inside, climbed up on the foot of my parents' bed, and giddily told them all about my first car date. They were very concerned about Paul. They were more concerned about their daughter's sadistic sense of humor.

He called when he got home that night to tell me what a great time he had. I laughed. Then he begged me to never tell anyone what had happened. I promised … then I laughed some more!

Sometimes in the journey of life, nature just calls. When it hits you, it hits you. By the time I was eighteen and he was twenty, we realized that maybe our crush had just been a pit stop and that our roads were taking us in different directions. It was painful for both of us.

Giving your heart away is easy; retrieving it rarely is. Somehow when your heart comes back, it is never in the same condition as when it was shared. Years have passed, and yet Paul still holds a place in my heart. I think of him sometimes and quietly laugh at the friendship we shared and the silliness we discovered. I pray that his wife is more compassionate than I and that she can handle puke.

As for my own daughters, I am praying that they can hold off on their own "potty breaks" of love for a while longer.

A Lady I Shall Be

All of my life an emphasis has been put on the whole concept of being a lady. I call it a concept because I never really saw it as a tangible thing. I checked and rechecked, and there was no location called "Lady Land" on my map. The lack of direction made it difficult for me to visualize what being a lady was or why I needed to become one.

As small children, my older brother, David, my younger sister, Ellen, and I were taught good manners. Ellen and I even received instruction through a week-long program called nothing less than "White Gloves and Party Manners."

The goal of the program was to produce fine ladies and gentlemen who would grow up to be, well, fine ladies and gentlemen. It was really a bit overwhelming as I think back on it. Imagine a bunch of seven-year-old children sitting around learning how to introduce the Queen of England to the mayor while dressed in clothes that itched.

I will admit that I have met a mayor or two over the years. But my ability to properly introduce the Queen has yet to be tested outside the classroom. I have become very experienced at wearing clothes that itch however.

I always felt like a bit of a contradiction where manners are concerned. On the one hand I loved black patent leather shoes; in fact they are the only shoes I wore as a young lady of eight. I never noticed the other children climbing trees and wading through the creeks were not wearing such fashionably flashy footwear.

On the other hand, there were things that were crystal clear. Like, one should not smack large wads of fruity bubble gum while enjoying a performance of *The Nutcracker*, especially not while seated next to the mother who sent you to "White Gloves and Party Manners."

To this day, I recall the look of horror that crossed my mother's face as she turned toward me and glared while the Sugar Plum Fairy pranced across the stage and I smacked along merrily. Brows creased in silent disapproval, she reached carefully and with great dignity into her purse and held out a fine white hankie with delicate little embroidered flowers on one corner.

Nothing was said. I knew instinctively that either I would place my gum into the hankie or Christmas would bypass my house that year. She still communicates volumes with those eyes.

As I became a teenager, it seemed like the contradictions in my world became starker. And something terrible happened to my parents. One minute they were cool, and the next they were not.

At school, it was the same way. I quickly realized that few—OK none—of my friends had gone to any sort of manners school, and the loss did not seem to cause them serious concern.

Of course, they did not know all the wonderful things they were missing. But if they had missed something so important, I reasoned, could it be that I had missed out on some vital experience as well? Was there some secret to happiness as a teenager that everyone else already knew? Had I missed the class on cool?

I decided to do some research. I became an observer. What was the difference between them and me?

One day, I stood by my locker and was amazed at the sea of denim that crowded the hallway.

That night at dinner, I could not wait to share the news with my family. I knew they would appreciate and benefit from the wisdom that I had gleaned from the halls of education. My brother, who had always worn jeans, just rolled his eyes at me. My sister, however, who was six years younger, seemed to share my excitement. When she got up to get more ice tea I was stunned to notice she was already outfitted in her own Calvin Klein's.

"Mother," I whined, like only a fourteen-year-old can. "Am I the only person in the world who doesn't own a pair of jeans?"

Without blinking, she dryly replied, "Of course not, dear, ladies do not wear jeans." There it was again, that lady concept.

I felt like this ghostly ideal would haunt me for the rest of my life if I did not somehow stand up and let it know who would define *me*. So with great power, I pushed myself away from the table and declared bravely, "Well, I am getting a pair of jeans!"

My parents just looked at each other like I was speaking a different language, shrugged their shoulders, and went on with dinner.

My mother, being the saint that she is, took me shopping that Saturday. It was a big day for me. I was going to my first boy-girl party that night, and I was getting a pair of jeans that day. Life was grand. We had always been department store shoppers, but that day, I discovered the inside of the mall. It was a small mall, but a girl has to start somewhere. There were plenty of trendy shops that carried every kind of denim, and I made it my personal mission to visit every one.

By day's end I had not only a pair of straight-legged jeans but a cool ecru-colored gauze shirt with pull strings on the shoulders and a skinny leather belt. Honey, I was hot.

As my mother drove me to the party, she gave me last-minute tips and suggestions that I had not learned in any party course.

1. Do not pair off. People will talk.

2. Do not cuss. It's tacky.

3. Do not smoke anything or drink liquor or beer. It is illegal.

4. Arrive late and make an entrance.

5. Leave early. It makes you alluringly unavailable.

She summed it all up by asking, "Have you got it? No drinking, no smoking, no fooling around." I had it all right; I had never experienced this side of the woman who was giving it to me, but I sure had it.

At the party, I tried my best to follow the rules. I really did. There was this one boy; however, who just would not leave me alone. He thought my jeans looked good. I know this because he told me at least a hundred times. He pestered me and thought himself to be cute. I thought him to be a cute pest. I guess at that age a cute pest was better than nothing.

Soon, my faithful parental coach arrived to return me and my jeans back home. Ironically, despite the attention, it felt comforting to be home and away from all the pressure of looking good for my new fan.

Monday morning came and with it came a new attitude, I sported my sassy new look to school. I wore a different shirt, of course, so that no one would think that, God forbid, I was wearing the same shirt twice.

All day long, I lingered in the halls between classes so that I could chat with everyone in the denim sea. It felt strangely different, but somehow good to be part of the crowd.

Just before lunch in a corridor crammed with what seemed like a million teenagers, a girl called my name loudly. I bounced as I turned around and innocently replied, "yes?"

Before me stood a beautiful young girl with dark curly hair that would have made the makers of electric rollers and VO5 hair spray proud of their achievements. Her eyeliner was an intense blue and was at least an inch thick. Despite her heavy makeup and stiff hair, or the fact that she smelled like a giant cigarette, she was quite pretty.

I had plenty of time to examine her closely because she stared at me for the longest minute of my life. Two things were running through my mind at that moment. First, who was this girl, and why was she standing in front of me like she wanted to beat me up and take my milk money?

Second, are those jeans painted on? They were the tightest things I had ever seen. She was not particularly big by any stretch, but she must not have known there were dressing rooms at the mall. Poor girl, no wonder she was frowning, she could not possibly breathe in those pants. I did not want to think about the wedgie she must have.

Her yelling derailed my train of thought and brought my attention back. Actually, it was more like screaming. The million people crammed into the corridor made a breathing circle around us. This was not exactly the kind of attention I had been aiming for.

I stood frozen as this girl verbally jackhammered me with words of which I am sure her mother would not have approved. Then, even more unexpectedly she lunged closer and told me and half of Alabama that I had stolen her boyfriend at the party on Saturday night and that now she would "kick my butt."

Two thoughts flashed through my mind. First, I would not brag that the little pest was my boyfriend, much less fight over him. Second, from the way she looked and the way she behaved, I knew that this girl was no lady. The revelation hit me.

With the poise of every grand lady that had gone before me, I wiped the stunned look off my face and said in the deep stage whisper that causes my accent to become a bit more pronounced, "I do not fight. I am a lady."

A hush fell over the hall of denim. I extended my head as high as my little neck would allow and turned away from her. With my face pointing upwards I glided down the hall, trying to look more confident than I felt. Secretly, I was certain that she was going to come up from behind at any moment and send my lady-like attitude flying through the air.

But I kept those thoughts and fears to myself. Later I learned that everyone had continued to stare silently at me as I disappeared, and then they had looked back to the angry young woman. The poor thing had been caught off guard so badly that it took her five minutes to come up anything else to say. By then the bell had rung, and everyone had pretty much moved on.

During my next class I asked the teacher if I could be excused to go to the restroom. I just needed a private moment. In the haven of the ladies' room I reached into my purse to get out a compact but instead pulled out a little, linen hankie with flowers embroidered on the corner. At that moment I knew who I was and who I was not. There was nothing wrong with jeans, but the fact was undeniable that I would always be more comfortable in black patent leather.

I realized that some destinations don't have to be visible to be tangible, and the best way to get to our destinations is to follow the compass within.

WHAT'S IN A NAME?

My mother was raised in the 1950s, when young girls, especially in the South, were given double names like Peggy Sue and Mary Linda. She was named Martha Glenn.

I have a personal theory on the best way to test all potential children's names. You go to your back porch and yell loudly, "Martha Glenn! Come to dinner!"

If it rolls gently off the land and comes back to you gracefully, it is yours to keep. If it lands with a thud, it was never yours to begin with. Martha Glenn is not a name that came back with ease.

At the peak of her insecurity as a teen, she lamented to her best friend. At the wise old age of seventeen, her friend Sharon responded, "Well, Martha, you are named after both your mother and your father, right?"

"Yes, Martha after my mom, Martha Marie, and Glenn after my dad, Larry Glenn."

"Well, what are you whining about? They could have named you Larry Marie!"

Sometimes in life, we just need perspective. Maybe things are not exactly as we wish, but considering all the possibilities, life could be a lot worse.

COUNT YOUR BLESSINGS

You know the saying, "Count Your Blessings?" Well, what if we all did? What if we all took thirty minutes every morning at 7:00 AM just to count, one by one, all the blessings in our lives?

Would the earth wobble on its axis? Would the heavens rumble to hear so much praise and thanksgiving at one time? What if in heaven there are one or two seriously great multi-tasking angels who get to flow all the praise to our Father's ears, and if we all began to thank Him at the same time, we might accidentally overwhelm the heavenly staff.

What a fun thought. One morning as I was saying good morning to the Lord, which is my custom, I thought of how grateful I am for my daughter, Bethany, and how proud I am of her as she gets older. I began to think about Allyson and thank God for her, and then I began to thank Him for Kara and Jeffrey and Jeff and so on and on. Then I realized I had said more than just good morning.

If my husband, Jeff, thought to wake me up one morning with a shower of praise and appreciation, I think I would have a seriously good day.

Can you imagine the noise we could make in heaven if we all just said thank you? Can you imagine the effect it would have in our lives if we all gave thanks? Let us all overwhelm heaven with gratitude, today.

BE YOU

I heard someone say once that children are pure.

If you want to remember who you really are you should think back to yourself in your earliest memory. Mine makes me laugh.

When I was about four, I got saved. I was so excited; I remember telling absolutely everyone what had happened to me. I remember singing in the beautiful Methodist church that I had the "joy, joy, joy down in my heart."

I also remember a nice old lady who used to stand by the coca-cola machine, telling me that I should try not to bounce while I sing. How can one sing about joy without bouncing? And what purpose would have one to sing without joy?

Over the years, I have owned the revelation that I cannot sing without bouncing and that I cannot deny the well of joy within me. It may annoy the sweet old ladies who stand by the coke machines of life, but that is OK.

Some choose to stand by the refreshments, and some choose to *be* refreshment. Be what you are. Be who you were at four.

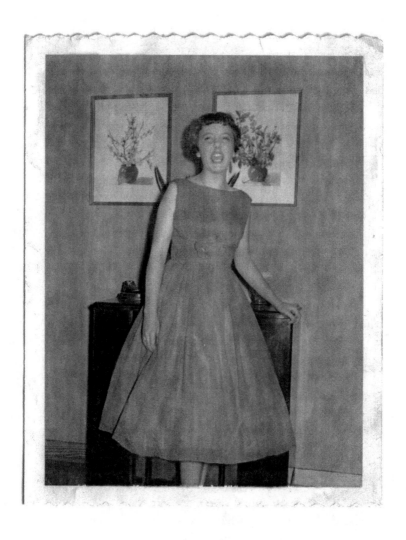

2

EASTER SHOES

Nowhere in the history of the church is it written that before one **can** celebrate Easter one must buy new shoes. I think a shoe salesman started this, years ago. A childless shoe salesman at that.

Just three short months after my birthing marathon producing four children in less than five years, the sun began to peak out of the winter clouds, and I knew spring must be coming. With great anticipation I awaited the benefits of warm weather and young children. That is when it hit me. If spring is almost here, then Easter is near as well.

As the first three of my children were female, I knew that there was only one place to begin celebrating the spring season: the mall. It is not cultural, it is not regional; it is inborn. Somehow my daughters just knew that there were dresses to be bought and shoes to be chosen.

My son, three months old at the time, was just happy to be there. With little forethought I packed my industrial-size diaper bag and made the troops ready. Diapers changed? Check! Gone to potty? Check! Clean shirts? Check! Hair bows in? Check!

Then I went through the same list for myself, poured a coke for me in a to-go cup, buckled four angels in four large car seats, and I was off!

Off my rocker! Have you ever tried to maneuver through a crowded mall with four children under five? How many twin strollers can one woman push?

"Are we done yet?"

"Can we go home now?"

"I'm ready for nap time."

These were the pleas that serenaded me almost as soon as we set out on the journey!

My oldest daughter's foot was too wide, my second daughter's foot too narrow. Every store we went into, we were greeted by what I call "gooners." They are curious people who cannot stop staring at the poor lady pushing two twin strollers. I had already become somewhat used to the typical reaction from people, which was, "Boy, you have your hands full."

I had my response memorized. I practiced regularly. I would slowly smile at the commenter, look lovingly at my children and genuinely reply, "Why yes, we are very blessed." This particular day as we pushed through the shoe search-a-thon, things were no different. The first thirty times or so, I was composed and congenial.

Several hours later, I sported baby spit-up in my hair and down my left shoulder. My snack-filled zippy bags were all empty, and the juice was all gone. So was my patience.

As I staggered through the bustling corridors, I was almost to the last store and my last hope. Then the miracle happened. Like a thirst-starved woman in the desert, I saw a mirage. In the distance, just beyond the fountain, I saw the most beautiful woman I had ever seen. It was my mother.

She had been out of town on business and had just run into the mall on her way home. With a look of bewilderment she asked me, "What in the world are you doing here alone?"

Mustering up all my remaining strength, I explained about shoes, girls, malls, and Easter. She took pity on me and offered to help us through the last store. I agreed, gratefully.

As we entered the store we were greeted by the usual smile and then the usual, "Oh my! Surely, they aren't all yours?" the clerk enquired as she peered judgmentally over the trendy glasses perched on her sharp little nose.

"For heaven's sake, don't you know where they come from?" the clerk continued.

That is when it happened. It was as if I was Charlie Brown in a classroom, because all I could hear was *wah wa-wa wah*. The room started to spin and I felt faint. Suddenly I could hear someone answering the saleslady's question. The words seemed to be coming from my mouth, unfortunately without stopping by my brain first.

"Yes," I proclaimed proudly. "These beloved children are all mine. Or at least they will be soon. After the paperwork is complete."

Out of the corner of my eye, I saw my mother's eyes popping out of her head in astonishment. I was undeterred, "And as far as where they came from," I continued, "We are well aware of the tragedy involved with their parents' untimely death. But being a saintly woman, out of the goodness of my heart, I will raise these precious babes as my own!" I continued shouting as my mother dragged those four babies and me to the decorative fountain out in the mall.

People looked at me in awe. There was a new reverence and compassion that oozed from shoppers. Suddenly all kinds of gooners were offering to help me.

My sweet mother, patting my hand, apologetically told everyone that I was not well and that she could handle it from there. With great tenderness she packed me, my industrial-size diaper bag, and the four babies into our mini van and followed us home. I think she put me to bed; I am sure she fixed dinner for my family.

Later that night, I was so grateful for the blessing of my mother. I realized that all those people at the mall must have missed out. I came to the sad conclusion that they had obviously never experienced the deep bond that can only be built through experiences like shopping for Easter shoes with your mother, no matter how old the child or the state of their mental health.

SUCCESS IS NEVER FINAL

Anyone who does not believe the truth of "success is never final" has never had curly hair, multiple children, or a desperately needed nap. Just when you think you have crossed the finish line, it all starts over.

I want to be successful; I want to know that I "Am" successful. Unfortunately for most of us, the Am-ing is harder than the going-to-be. When we were children, people asked us what we wanted to be when we grew up. They never asked us what we were in the present. That is so frustrating. Why don't we ask six-year-olds what they are?

Because they would say, "I'm a girl. Duh."

But when we grow up we suddenly have to "Be." We have to Be engaged, and then we have to Be married. Then we have to Be a mom, Be a wife, Be a friend, Be a sister, Be a savior blah, blah, blah.

And even that is never enough. Just about the time you get engaged and say, "I Am getting married," everyone wants to know when you will Be married. After marriage the question looms of when will you Be parents and so on. There is no rest for weary sojourners just trying to get the hang of Am-ing.

I have friends who did not take the beaten path that everyone else so gladly tramples. They have remained single, or childless. Some have even remained careerless and yet they are still functioning members of society. Imagine that.

Success is never final. I know this because I have put my kids to bed clean only for them to wake up dirty. I have sold homes only to need to sell more the next month. I have taught a Bible study only to forget everything.

One day, very recently, I woke up and I was forty. No one seems to ask me what I want to Be anymore, and yet I Am.

Had I known no one cared, I might have made different choices. Probably not, but possibly. It is rather liberating, really, to think that my success is now on my timeline and not that of others. I suppose I am glad we accomplished my husband's dream to-do list first after all. Now I can enjoy the Am that God has called me to Be.

WERE YOU A P.W.W.O—E, S OR U?

Which did you get in school? You know "Plays Well With Others:" *E* for Excellent; *S* for Satisfactory; or *U*, well, U name it and that is what U is for: Undesirable, Unsuitable, Unsatisfactory, or did you ever cop the Unintentional excuse with your mom?

This important life question was posed for me one day when my husband was trying to describe someone who frustrated him. When he could not get his thoughts and his words to coincide, he just looked at me and said, "Doesn't Play Well with Others."

I, of course, knew exactly the type person my hubby was describing. In fact I saw a man take a parking place quickly at Wal-Mart the other day when another car was clearly waiting politely to get the spot, and I thought, "Oh, there ya go. I bet he definitely got a *U!*"

You see it all over. Some people are team players, and some people are not. Or maybe they are just not willing to get along for some reason.

Which makes me ponder further, what was the point of grading us on that in first grade anyway? Did it help anyone? Was it just to separate the *U*s from the *S*s from the *E*s?

I was always an *E*. I cannot remember even getting an *S*. Conduct was another subject altogether, but we shall not go there as the pain is still too fresh. My hand just did not rise as fast as my mouth started moving. It is probably a medical condition that has yet to be officially named—but I digress.

Anyway, as Jeff and I lamented his unfortunate encounter, we realized that we were both *E*s who had been blessed to find each other. And that in perking-along on this journey, we needed to have grace for the *S* people and especially the *U* people, no matter how much they perplex us.

Maybe that's why they graded us after all. Maybe it was so that we could hook up with our own kind, which would validate the importance of this otherwise random-seeming rambling.

To those who have not yet found a partner for the journey, choose wisely. Be sure and ask your friends too. After all, it is no fun trying to play with people who never learned how to play well others.

TRANSPARENT HALLWAYS

Jeffrey hides under the coffee table. Ashley thinks that she is Miss Priss. We made a gumdrop tree. The clock only dings on the hour. Mom wears purple gloves. Allyson sucks her thumb and smells her blankey. Maga is spending Christmas with us. I like Little House on the Prairie. *Dad likes to eat nuts. Kara likes to play with dolls. Mom got a beautiful stuchue* (she probably meant statue …) *We get to open presents, and we are dog-sitting.*

Once, a very long time ago, 1994 to be exact, my now eighteen-year-old wrote this as her diary entry. I loved it so much I cut it out, framed it, and have it hanging in my hallway. Hallways are usually just the in-between; passageways that connect one place we want to be with another. It is pretty ordinary to hang pictures of our family in these in-between spaces of our homes. I chose to hang a diary excerpt.

I have asked myself many times as I have passed by this framed memory, "What would happen if we posted pages from our journals in our hallways?" If we were brave enough, or crazy enough, to post these for the world to see our inner thoughts, captured like a snapshot of a season in our lives? Bethany's journal excerpt definitely does that. It seems it was only yesterday that she was five and already observing her world.

The same hallway that once connected some bedrooms and bathrooms to the rest of the house now operates more like a time capsule, but with the power of a challenge. It reminds me that children are only small for a day and that I should desire to be so transparent. My heart should be so pure that my thoughts could be posted on a hallway wall.

When I was a child, I remember wondering if when I saw Jesus if he was going to tell all of my sins, bad thoughts, and deeds. As I grew up I realized that that was not the case, of course, and that life is like a hallway. It is merely the transition that delivers us to eternity, a beautiful and memorable journey but really just a connecting point to "the rest of the house."

Be transparent.

PICTURE THIS

I have thirty-five family photo albums, seventy-five thousand pictures in boxes and 263 framed snapshots around my house. So far.

I like pictures. I like to have a camera with me so I can be ready to capture every memory. Usually I miss the amazing moments, but luckily my family is gracious enough to stop experiencing the moment and recreate the moment for me to capture.

A few years back when I was at the peak of my scrapbooking craze, a friend pointed out that I was only present twice in the album that I had just finished, which beautifully and creatively displayed our year as a family.

"I was there," I explained, "I was the one taking the pictures. That's why I am not in any of them."

"So you were watching your family's life this past year?" Her words stung.

That night as I went to bed, I asked my husband if he had noticed that I was not in any of the albums.

"You hate to have your picture taken, that's why you take all the pictures," he said matter-of-factly.

Double ouch! He expected me not to be in any pictures. I lay in bed, thinking how easy it would be to replace me. My children were young enough that they could probably forget me, and, since there were no Kodak reminders, it would not be that hard.

I thought about dying and being replaced. How easy it would be for the next wife to come right into my home and cut my face out of the only two pictures in the album and glue her face in instead. How dare she? And it would be all because I was not thrilled with my image.

The vain reality hit me that I can either experience the journey or buy a boxed seat and enjoy the view from above. I still take pictures, but so do all of my children. Now when I scrapbook, I try my best to capture all who were present.

I don't want to watch life; I want tangible reminders that I lived it.

GIVE

Give and it will be given unto you. A good measure, pressed down, shaken together and running over, will be poured out on your lap. For with the measure you use, it will be measured to you.

—*Luke 6:38 (NIV)*

My mother believes that you can buy items to give to others, but they are only items until you give them away; it is then they become gifts. Along those same lines, she believes that spiritual gifts or the talents we possess are not gifts for ourselves at all but, rather, are merely good qualities we posses until we give them away by using them to serve someone else.

God gave us all talents. Granted, we cannot all become the next American Idol or make our debut on Broadway, but we all have gifts. Some do everyday things exceptionally well, like cook or decorate or garden. Some people are able to stand up in front of people and articulate a clear vision, while some are able to sit on very small chairs and read to children. Some encourage; some entertain; some inspire; some reassure; some nurture; some instruct; and yet all of these things are gifts.

Gifts are to be given, shared, poured out, and lavished on others. At the very least, they are to be given. If we hold them to ourselves, our talents bless no one and will eventually wither and die. If we use our gifts to bless others we discover our own road becomes more tolerable and our own burdens lighten.

So cook some banana bread for a friend, send a teacher an encouraging note, sing in church, whatever you can do. Give. Give, and it will be given to you pressed down and shaken together, and running over.

IS MY LIFE A LEMONADE STAND?

I love it when I meet someone new and they ask, "Soooo, what do you do?"

Certainly I can say that I am a realtor, or a mom, or a wife, or a pastor's wife, or this, or that, but what I really want to tell them is "I give." What would happen if we all started saying that?

"Hey, what do you do?"

"Oh, I give. I am a giver of encouragement and refreshment."

One day, driving passed some children proudly selling lemonade in their yard, I wondered: if my life was a lemonade stand is there a price for those who are refreshed by me, or is it free? I mean, think about it. Do we trade with people?

Do you expect that if I scratch your back, you will scratch mine? Do we indebt others to us? "I have done so much for you, and now I am calling in my chips. You owe me big time." Or do we just give freely? Some weeks rank up there in giving. In fact, sometimes I wonder if there will be anything left to give the next day or to the next person.

It is during those times that I have found the need to keep an inventory check on my heart. I do not want to be a bitter lemonade lady who resents the sourness that life has squeezed my way. And I do not want to just give away sugar water, lacking the substance of what I am called to give. I want to keep on growing until my life is a drink offering to the body of Christ, as well as to my King.

What would happen if we all just gave?

THE PARABLE OF THE BETTER BERRY

Once upon a time there was a better berry.

It was planted in a garden of berries and hidden among the millions, all so similar in many regards. One day the gardener came along with his basket, and the better berry knew it was time for harvest. Better Berry swelled with delight as the gardener passed by and was pleased as he was picked off his vine. Instantly he found himself in a basket with other berries, some smaller, some larger, but he himself knew it to be true and that he was indeed … better.

As the gardener approached his truck, the Better Berry found himself sorted into a basket of ripe and delicious berries much like him. He knew his destiny was before him and that it was great. A loud noise startled him as he found himself bouncing down a conveyer belt. *This must be a mistake,* he thought as he drew closer to a large metal device. Within minutes he was de-seeded, de-juiced, preservatives were added, and he was pressed beyond recognition.

"How will I top the cake?" he screamed inwardly. No one heard.

Instead he was stretched out, rolled up, and packaged into a fruit roll-up and thrown into some ungrateful child's lunchbox, only to be traded for a Twinkie.

Sometimes the destiny I have planned doesn't exactly work out. During my own process of being de-seeded and de-juiced and pressed beyond recognition, I have to remember that there is a greater plan for my life than being a cake topper.

Some days I am OK with that, and some days I am not. At the end of all days, the Better Berry was enjoyed as he was pulled apart and shared on a playground, probably by many more children than could ever have been delighted in him as a topper.

Life is not always what we think it will be. The secret is to trust the gardener.

3

GAZE IN THE RIGHT DIRECTION

One January, I had a dream that I was sitting in a coffee shop, looking at the bottom of an empty, stained cup when I heard a voice. It said, "Turn your gaze."

When I did, I saw another table to my left that I had not noticed before. It had dozens of full cups of coffee stacked on top of each other. Then I heard the words, "Measure gain." I woke up.

Needless to say this had an impact on me. Amazingly, everywhere I turned that year, I found I was measuring my gain and marveling at the abundance of our Lord.

Sometimes we have to be told to shift our gaze. We get stuck spending our time focusing on the empty and the stain, when our father in heaven has a table set with abundance ready for us. We just have to turn our gaze.

Note to self: gaze up.

DIRECTION SIGNS

Have you ever thought about detours on the journey of life? You know how sometimes you think you are perking along on the right road and suddenly you see the guy standing with his belly hanging out, holding one of those "ROAD-WORK AHEAD" signs, and before you know it you have been detoured.

It would be nice if God would just send a belly-baring angel into our lives to trumpet a sign that says, "HEART WORK AHEAD."

At least then we would all be prepared for what lies ahead. Instead, we often find ourselves caught by surprise and yet oddly familiar with the routine. Then we mutter the infamous words that we have all muttered: "not this again," or "can anything else bad happen?"

Recently on a real life road detour, I discovered a road I had never been on. I was scared since it was poorly marked, and I was not familiar with the area at all. I was sure I was going to get lost and waste a bazillion dollars in gas and time. But I did not. Low and behold a few days later some homebuyers came in from out of town, and when I laid out the course of houses they were to see, I discovered that little road connected them all without the hassle of the interstate—pretty handy really.

I think that is what God really wants to impart to us. Some roads scare us and are not our preference. They may even require a faith that we don't think we possess. But He is the great GPS and He will not let us get lost. So the best thing for us to do is to simply posture ourselves the best we can for the detour and ask the Lord to teach us a new way along the journey.

Who knows, it may just eliminate the detours, at least the ones teaching us those lessons anyway. God really does love to work all things, even our roads of frustration, together for good because He is for them that love Him and who are called according to His purposes.

Movin' on

If your past dominates your present, then it will predict your future.

As a young youth minister not too long after we were married, my husband was working on a sermon for the youth of our church. He was talking it out as if I were invisible in our bedroom. This was a customary practice, so I did not mind.

He said the above words in a disconnected way—just thoughts floating through the air.

Bam! It hit me. He had hit upon one of those simple, life-changing truths. Quickly I jumped up to my feet in the middle of our bed and, wearing my most soulful expression and bouncing up and down on the mattress, I preached to the preacher.

"IF … YOUR … PAST … DOMINATES … YOUR … PRESENT … IT … WILL …" I shouted between bounces, "… IT … WILL … PREDICT … YOUR … FUTURE!"

He preached that message from the pulpit the following Wednesday, and it was good. We have preached that message to one another for the last fifteen years, and it has changed our life together.

Lay it down; move on.

U-TURNS ALLOWED

Life is about choices. I have heard that maxim my whole life. But my love of justice always struggled with this declaration. Not because I did not believe it to be true, but because I have traveled enough to have seen people "with" and those "without," and it seemed both resulted from very few choices.

I have a niece-by-marriage, Betty, who is also a best friend by choice. We have loved each other since we met in the early 1980s. I watched her put herself through pharmacy school, deal with the usual issues of becoming an adult, give birth to four beautiful daughters, and help a husband survive medical school. She is amazing.

Betty was raised in California. She lived across the hall from my brother-in-law and his wife in a very bad apartment complex. Betty's mother was an alcoholic and was less than fit as a parent and had lost several other children to child services. Betty herself was regularly in and out of foster care.

My in-laws kept an eye out for Betty, and when her mother would fail to come home for days at a time, leaving only cereal on the table for the seven-year-old, Betty would stay with them as well. Years later, after my in-laws moved back to Tennessee, Betty's mother called to see if they could watch Betty for few days while she honeymooned with her new eighteen-year-old husband. They agreed. Basically, she never came back. They registered her into her freshman year of high school with no idea where her mother was or if she was even alive.

Years ago we were pregnant together, her with her first child, me with my third. It was a wonderful season to be able to share with one another. Until one of those defining moments changed everything.

Being pregnant always brings your own mothering issues to the forefront, whether they are real or not. There was no exception for Betty. During her first pregnancy, she received the fateful call saying that her mother was passing and asking if Betty could come to California before she was gone.

She did not want to. She cried and rationalized a hundred reasons why she should not go. Her husband was a precious support, and in the end, they made the journey together. Betty made it out there in time, and her mother even asked for forgiveness from her deathbed. I remember the pain in Betty's voice as she told me how it felt like "too little, too late."

While in California, Betty also saw her best friend from childhood, who had become a prostitute. She went to see her old home, which had been overrun by drug dealers. From this experience, she understood in a new way the words, "But for the grace of God, this would have been me."

It would have been easy for her to return to her comfortable new home and beautiful furnishings and pretend that none of it had ever happened. But, epiphanies are divine interventions to direct our paths.

When her mother did pass away, she received a check in the mail. Astonished she called to tell me that a check had come for a couple thousand dollars from her mother's estate. She could not believe it. The bitterness poured out of her as she remembered struggling to support herself through pharmacy school and how life had been so unfair to her for so long. She said she was going to use the money to pay down her college loans.

I paused with a revelation of my own. "Betty, don't do it," I said. "Take that money and buy the inheritance that you would have wished for."

"What?" she asked incredulously.

"Make a U-turn with your heritage. You can't help where you have come from but you can help where you are going. Go buy something extravagant that you have always wanted, like a grandfather clock. And put one of those little brass plaques on the back that says something like, 'given in love' by your mother. If life could have been the way you would have chosen you would be inheriting wonderful antiques and beautiful memories."

"Your past was not about your choice, but your future is. So go buy something that declares beauty because that is what God has done for you. He has exchanged beauty for ashes. And every time your own children ask where you got such a fine piece of craftsmanship you should declare, as if into the heavens, it is my inheritance and yours!"

Betty did just that. She thought the plaque on the back was a little too much, but she loved the idea of a grandfather clock. It is marvelous—magnificent even. Sometimes in life others set our course, but that does not mean we have to stay on it. U-turns are allowed.

Sometimes we find ourselves driving down the road and wondering how in the world we got so lost. When you realize you are headed in the wrong direction, do not be afraid that someone will criticize you for being wrong or lost in the past. Just make a U-turn, and everything will be all right.

ALL WASHED UP

Some days I feel like a washcloth that has been left on the counter all day. The corners feel parched and drawn, free from moisture or purpose. There is a hint of past accomplishment and a hint of destiny to come. But in the present, there is a parched, drawn cloth that has been rung out.

There is a time for everything. I will not stay here forever. I will spend some time; because sometimes we just have to rest alone for what lies ahead.

AS IT IS IN HEAVEN

Have you ever been driving down the road and the sun suddenly blinds you as you make a turn? Your eyes water, you strain to see the road, and despite the fact that you know the general direction you are traveling, you are suddenly dangerously close to wrecking. All because of a little vision impairment.

The same is true on our spiritual journey. We perk along, and even though we have a basic knowledge of the direction we are headed, we find ourselves so easily blinded and unable to see the road ahead.

In my prayers lately, the words I hear over and over are "as it is in heaven, let it be done on earth." Of course these are some of the words Jesus uttered as he prayed in what we refer to as "The Father's Prayer."

What hinders us from seeing things from heaven's perspective? What hinders from seeing His perfect will for something, or someone? Or even ourselves?

Jesus prayed with knowledge that there was a perspective other than His own, and so should we. Then it hit me that we just need to put on our Son-glasses.

Cheesy, I know. But yes, Son-glasses.

If we could just put His lenses over our own, then surely the little things that usually hinder us would seem less dangerous or life-threatening. Then we would stay on His course with confidence, sure of our destiny and purpose.

GRATITUDE WILL GET YOU EVERY TIME

Live in the space of gratitude. I read that in an article once, and I keep thinking about it. The article further said that when we are in a place of need, what we really need is the gift that gratitude gives us, which is perspective.

Perspective when we are full is so much different from when we are hungry. Perspective when we are loved, have money in the bank, or a new car is always different from when we lack. Yet all we have to do is cultivate and live in gratitude to lend ourselves perspective when we need it the most.

Shortly after I began pondering this, a realtor that I was working on a transaction with shorted me out of two thousand smackaroos. He lied, bottom line, and I lost.

Oddly, it happened the same day that a client that had a listing with another company called little ol' me and wanted to switch to me because she had heard good things about my character.

I love gentle reminders from the Lord that living in the space of gratitude brings rewards. My own ungratefulness was limiting my ability to see what blessing was waiting for me with the next house I was to list. I bet most days are like that for all of us.

Let us live in the space of gratitude today, and get a new perspective on life.

GREETED BY GRATITUDE

Though the fig tree does not bud and there are no grapes on the vines, though the olive crop fails and the fields produce no food, though there are no sheep in the pen and no cattle in the stalls, yet I will rejoice in the Lord, I will be joyful in God my Savior. The sovereign Lord is my strength, he makes my feet like the feet of a deer, he enables me to go on to new heights.

—Habakkuk 3:17–19 (NIV)

One morning when I woke up the funniest thing happened. My lungs compressed exhaling completely and then enlarged drawing in so much more. I am speaking of air of course but that first great yawn also awakened me to joy.

Whenever gratitude greets me so early in the day with the gentle reminder that even though life is weird, people are weird and paychecks are often too late or too small, God is Good.

I was reminded of Scarlet—yes, Scarlet in *Gone with the Wind*—in the scene where she is on a hill, overlooking the burning of Atlanta. There is nothing she can do about it. She loved Atlanta, and yet all she could do was watch it burn. Sometimes I feel like that about relationships in my life.

You invest, you love people, you work to establish a ministry or a job or whatever it is for you, and then you watch people around you self-destruct by making bad or wrong choices, you watch people hurt because others are making bad choices that affect them, you watch people act unethically in business or in life, and sometimes, most times in fact, I want to blow an invisible referee whistle and call time. Just to make everyone *stop.*

That morning, I was greeted by grace for the gift of life, without even asking. As I opened my eyes, I saw a little dust bunny clinging to my bedroom curtains. So I got up and, without a thought, brushed off the little clump of dust. As I did, the sun burst in through the window, and the scattering dust swirled in a thousand directions.

Giddiness filled my heart; I knew it was a greeting from the Lord saying, "My mercies are new every morning. And, the things that you think are debris are really just fruitless vines and fig trees not yet blossoming. They are temporary. You choose to praise me."

So with a tangible gratitude, I started that day and choose to start others with joy in my heart and Habakkuk 3:17–19 in my soul.

May you have a revelation day, filled with gratitude.

SELAH

You know what? Life can be confusing and crazy and a roller coaster ride and frustrating and fulfilling and peaceful, all in the same day.

I love the book of Psalms. I love it because, during the course of a day and while experiencing any of those emotions, I can meditate on a psalm and express my heart to our Father.

One of the words consistently used in that book is "Selah." You know why I love that word? Do this with me. Take a moment—go ahead; no one is watching—and breathe in as deeply as you can, then slowly exhale.

You just took in something you did not even know you needed and let go of something you thought you could not live without. Selah. Such a simple word keeps me centered in the ups and downs.

Father, I pray that you will rush into my spirit and fill me with even more than I think I need. I am asking for the more. Then remove from me all the gunk, opinions, thoughts, judgments, or minor irritations that I can live without. I want the more, selah.

I feel better. How 'bout you?

PEOPLE ARE NOT PAYCHECKS

People are not paychecks. They are just people.

One day I was talking with a new realtor who was confused about how he had calculated so carefully each person that he had been working with and placed a dollar amount on what they would provide for him. He was frustrated at how some of those potential clients had not come through for him.

I cautioned him, saying, "you know, people are not paychecks … they are just people."

Few of us actually look at one another as a means of acquiring literal wealth, but it is so easy to look at others as a means to meet our needs in other ways. We want others to hear the Lord for us. We want others to simply tell us which direction to take. We see people like paychecks, a means to fill a need or a deficit.

The epiphany here is that if we learn to let God be God and let his people just be his people reflecting Him, then I am confident we will receive His full blessing that is meant for us. Not the splenda substitute that we sometimes think is just as good.

The truth is that no one can give us the right directions because they do not hold the map. There is only one God who can meet all of our needs, and the really good news is that He meets those needs according to His riches and glory, not ours. Take an inventory of where your paychecks come from as well as to whom or what you are stretching out your hands.

People are not paychecks, they are just people.

THE INTERSECTION OF TIME AND SPACE

Chronos means literal or measurable time, and Kairos means a specific God-time or divine appointment. I believe that when we pray, "As it is in heaven, let it be done on earth," we are asking for heaven's time to meet with earth's time.

For instance, if I am faithful in my chronos by living presently and not in the past, for seizing all that He has for me this day, when his divine Kairos moments occur, I am able and ready to discern and receive them.

We all have those divine moments that occur, being in the right place at the right time. But I pray, "As it is in heaven let it be done on earth," because I do not want to miss a Kairos moment happening in my life now because I am distracted, living in the past, holding others in the past, or just living in la la land, dreaming of what I think life should be.

I want to be faithful in the chronos, so He will find me faithful to be blessed by seeing the two meet.

4

LUGGAGE LIMITS

As we travel through life, we need to stop and notice the little things. Or what should be little things. This is a topic of great weight and substance and probably a key to the very future of civilization as we know it. If you do not already, I hope you will soon agree with me. There should be a legal limit to the size of fanny packs.

Now please forgive the lack of spirituality here, but sometimes we have to address the practical things that can distract us from the spiritual. So, in some sense, this too has a spiritual goal.

You see I recently went to a book resale event and found myself in a sea of fanny-packed moms rolling around dollies of books. You know how you go to an event, and if you are helping, you have a pass around your neck to have full access? Well, obviously the pass in the book resale event world is the fanny pack.

I saw the Queen enter. She came in and all the busy worker bees stopped and took notice. I did as well. I could not help it, her fanny pack was as big as—well, let me just say it this way, Samsonite that was designed to be carry-on luggage should not be wrapped around someone's waist.

Furthermore, what could be going through the mind of any woman as she is wrapping large black Velcro straps around her already over-size waist? The tight belts create or even enlarge unsightly rolls across the lower back, which is unattractive enough, but having a suitcase squeezed in between the hips and gut? Only one of those unfortunate rail-thin bicycling enthusiasts could have ever thought this was a good idea.

I am not likely to recover from the trauma of this experience for some time. I am still aghast. Standing next to Queen Fanny for about ten minutes as we waited for our checks from the sale gave me ample time to study the design of said stumbling block and the person sporting it. Actually as I waited she held court. She could not have been taller than five feet and was what can only be described as fluffy. But whatever she had in that fanny pack, her subjects must have really wanted some for themselves.

Arriving home I asked my husband Jeff, "Shouldn't there be a law?"

I understand that it is handy to have a little bag of some sort to keep track of ones things while on the go. That is why early man created purses and backpacks. But fanny packs? They ought not to be allowed unless you are practicing for the Tour de France. But, regardless of the purpose, when they are as big as you are … well, my friends, that is just wrong.

So the next time you are tempted to strap a laptop to your waist, or you want to take a set of bongos along to the grocery store, or there is a covered dish dinner at your church and you feel like strapping a couple of casserole dishes to your stomach, just stop. Stop in the name of beauty and all that is good in this world. Stop, if for nothing else, for the good of the children.

The young are too impressionable and might glance up and see the power of Queen Fanny and mistakenly aspire to as much in their own lives. We must unite and set things right in the world.

OH CHRISTMAS TREE

Ah, the tree. The pursuit of the perfect one, the presentation of the new ornaments the whole process just makes Christmas ... Christmas.

Last year my family and I dressed in our matching red sweaters and trekked out to cut down the perfect tree. Just like Martha Stewart, we quickly found just the right one, complete with snow topping the branches. We held hands in a circle and sang Christmas carols and then easily chopped it down and dragged it home for the holidays.

Actually that is such a wish-filled lie! The truth is that my hubby, Big Jeffy was pooped from talking a hundred people over a crisis all day, and by the time we were finally all ready to go get the tree, he was having second thoughts.

First, he told me that we could just use the pre-lit six-footer that lives in the basement the other eleven months of the year. I looked devastated and proceeded to give him a rousing speech that would have made Martin Luther King Jr. proud (it would have been completely perfect if my kids had hummed *Oh Christmas Tree* in the background). Then he blamed the budget and everything else he could think of. Finally he resorted to, "Kathy, a live tree does not make Christmas."

I practice making shocked faces in a mirror, so the one I shared with him was very good.

"Nooooo, dahlin', it does not!" I said with my softest, deepest southern accent, trying to gain some sense of composure, "it makes the timeless memories that we treasure the rest of our lives."

He yielded.

Woo-hoo for yielding. Then he tried to pull a fast one and let the kids go get the tree without us. I lowered my brow. A look that I only whip out for the most serious offenses, but I figured this counted.

Once again, he yielded. So at last we all loaded up the van and began to sing and think happy thoughts. Woo-hoo for Christmas!

But instead of driving to *Toys "R" Us*, the place we normally go to buy our tree, and which second-born Allyson noted immediately, Big Jeffy got off on an unknown exit. This caused much anxiety for us all right away.

"Where are we going?"

"What are you doing, Dad?"

We drove on and on. I knew we were in trouble when I noticed that we were in an area that I have never been in before, at least not after dark. So I sweetly suggested, "Honey, I think we may be in the hood."

He said nothing. We passed a lingerie store the size of Wal-Mart and across from it was a sign over a store advertising Cheap Cigs. It was then that I knew we were in "The Hood."

I pressed the lock button in the car to dramatize my concern and still he said nothing. Perhaps he mumbled something about a budget and finally pulled over at a corner crowded with shivering little Christmas trees. The place had great trees at amazing prices and the fact that my children had to wear bullet proof vests and hide under the seats was perfectly worth the risks to get such a great deal on the perfect tree.

We left that lot with one very happy Big Jeffy.

The moral of this story is that bringing home a live tree does not make Christmas. But it does provide the priceless memories that we will all, uh, *treasure* forever.

PROPORTIONS
A revelation on aging …
or at least a trick of the trade.

On a recent visit to the hairdresser, I had the typical experience: sitting in the chair with soaking wet hair and that big black drape wrapped too tightly around my neck. I explained to my hairdresser that I wanted her to straighten my hair.

I tried not to look at my image in the mirrors all around me. My usual hairdresser was unavailable, so I visited someone new. She was young, tan, and beautiful so instead of looking at my soaking wet head with the too tight drape squishing my little neck, I contemplated her instead. I had no idea they were giving twelve year olds a license to cut hair.

She tried her best, pulling handfuls of hair tight with a comb and blowing them dry in a vain effort to get the whole mass to lay flat on my head as I had asked. I was born with very curly hair that prefers to poof out in every direction. It is not my fault.

The child-hairdresser stopped periodically to reorganize herself, first trying hair products from her own station and then running around to other stylists for backup. They would glance over, furrow their brow and nod, and then pass her some new product with helpful names like *Glue-it 'cause it won't smooth down*. She would run back over to me, apply the new goo and try blowing it out again and again and again.

At last she swiveled the chair around to reveal the outcome to me. As she stood back and looked at my short stubby neck, still draped too tightly in that black tablecloth, and my hair finally completely flat on my little pea-sized head, I think she felt sorry for me. I looked like an egg, fat side down.

Without further encouragement, she turned me back around and began to tease up the top of my hair. She nearly got carpal tunnel back-combing my mane.

As young as she was, she had just learned one of the most important, if unwritten, rules of hair. The farther the chin (or a second or third chin) hangs down as we age, the higher you are allowed to poof up the hair on the top of your head to create the illusion of balance.

She worked on my hair for a while and finally breathed a sigh of relief at the accomplishment. I am sure she was afraid that in the earlier state I would have been a walking warning to other women not to come to the salon.

It says in the Bible for the old women to teach the young; this is why. I am glad my poofy hair and tiny head were there to provide the inspiration for her epiphany. Undoubtedly, many other women of a certain age have benefited from the lesson learned that day.

STRETCH MARKS

Do you know why we get stretch marks? We get them because God's divine plan is for us to use them as tools. OK, maybe this is not exactly a traditional doctrine, but hear me out.

Everyday when we get dressed, we are reminded that we traded vanity—and our futures as swimsuit models—in order to bring life to this earth.

And every day that our children act a fool, we can say, "do you really think that I sacrificed my gorgeous, young body in order for you to go around acting like you have no mama? I don't think so!"

And everyday when we undress, we can be reminded that life is not all about us. Not even close.

LIKE A STRING AROUND MY FINGER

Quite a few years ago, my husband brought me a bracelet from a mission trip to a remote area of Russia that desperately needed the Good News.

At the time, I had only two thoughts on my mind. First, I was glad that he was back. Second, I was mad that he had been gone for two weeks without a word to let me know whether he was safe or even alive.

Back then, we did not have e-mail or cell phones, and when people were gone, they were just gone. It was during that time that I, being six months pregnant with our fourth child, went into premature labor and was relegated to bed rest. Imagine his surprise when he came home to that! And while the bracelet was nice, it just did not fill the emotional need I felt at that time. In truth, I resented the bracelet a little. It reminded me of that hard season.

Quite a few years later, a couple that had been led to the Lord and was now pastoring a church in that far-off country as a result of Jeff's trip visited the states and came to see us. As they shared their story with our church, I wept. I wept and wept, actually. I was moved to tears not by their words, their testimonies, or even their journey, but rather by my own selfishness.

Despite my fear and resentment at being left alone during the pregnancy, I had not lost my son, and in fact, as God had promised, I had given birth to a healthy boy. I had not worn that bracelet, I had not prayed about these feelings or for those struggling to bring the word to Russia and other lands. By then, I barely even remembered that time of trial, and yet God had been faithful to me. My conviction that night was as strong as any I have ever known. I repented.

Sometimes we have to take inventory of our hearts and deal with the junk. Clearly God had asked me to be an intercessor for the nations, witnessed by the simple gift of a bracelet from my husband, and I had responded with selfishness. That night I realized how my behavior must have felt to the good Father who loves all of his children.

I began to wear that bracelet, and I began praying for the flock in Russia. The bracelet became a beautiful reminder to pray. And bracelets became our tradition. As Jeff traveled, he would bring back a new bracelet to remind us of all he had witnessed, and I committed each of them to prayer.

Now, years later I have a large box filled with prayers from around the world. When I get dressed each morning, I choose which nation to wear. I love it when children at church ask, "Miss Kathy, what country are you praying for today?" It brings me such joy to respond, "First, tell me why I wear this bracelet."

"Because it reminds you that we have sisters and brothers everywhere, and God loves them just as much as he loves us," they have learned to say. Every time I hear it, I smile in my heart.

I love it when I am complimented on one of these unique pieces of love and art at work or while shopping. It has become a beautiful way for me to share the love of a good Father with total strangers.

Sometimes extraordinary things happen during our ordinary days. We fail to take time to receive the gift or even to recognize the sign that God is giving us. But it is never too late to listen. What is He asking you to do? How has He reminded you that we are a part and not the whole?

Close your eyes, and let your heart remember. I guarantee you that a street sign is waiting to give you direction.

THE REALITY IS

If you have children, you have probably questioned your own sanity at some point. You have probably questioned God's as well, and wondered if He really is all-knowing then what was He thinking when he gave you children? Those thoughts have often strolled through my head anyway.

As a mother of four teenagers I have wondered where there is a book titled *When You Do It Right and Things Still Go Wrong*. Some days, I have more questions than answers.

I am a mom-mom. You know, the room mom, the mom on the field trip. I read my children books, taught them their colors, had daily craft time and play time and even scheduled their naps at different times so that I could have quality time with each. I am sure along the way I made errors or shut down because of fatigue, but now that they are suddenly on the eve of adulthood, I find myself ... back to more questions. I feel the nervousness that comes with time slipping too quickly through my hands.

What if I haven't taught them enough of the word of God? What if they are not sure enough of who they are to stand in the face of adversity? What if I haven't taught them to live a life of giving to others before themselves? My mother is a very wise woman, so I went to her with my questions.

"Kathy, did Adam and Eve have a perfect parent?" she asked.

"Well, yes," I wisely and slowly replied.

"Well dahlin' even with a perfect Father, look how they messed up. The good news is that that same perfect Father has a plan for your children too, and He is quite good at working everything out in the end."

The reality is everything works out in the end. If it hasn't worked out, you are not at the end. Luckily, neither am I.

ETERNITY

You know the phrase, "life is a journey not a destination?" I have been fascinated with the concept of this journey for some time. I enjoy pondering this journey and the next—the next, of course, being eternity.

What if eternity is a journey too? Are we going to get to heaven and whine to God, "but I want to see all of you now!" Like the girl in *Willy Wonka and the Chocolate Factory*, Veruca Salt, wanting everything now or else?

I am amazed at how impatient we can be on this miraculous journey. Maybe it is just me, but it is so easy to want more. I wanted to be married, and then I was married. I wanted a family and got that too. Yet, there are always more dreams and desires. I want to be this or that.

I am reminded of Mother Teresa. What a Godly woman. She was not always a mother. In the beginning, she was just a sister. I bet she set her heart on the pilgrimage and emerged slowly into the Mother known and loved by so many. I read an interview with her once in which she said that she was always surprised that she got any attention at all, not yet having accomplished all that she wanted. She was already getting up in years at that point, and she was still focused on the goal.

This type of thought always reminds me that we need fuel for the journey, which in this case is fruit … fruit of the spirit anyway. Self-control and patience, like apples and oranges, are two fruits in particular that leap to mind.

I suppose as I journey through this round here on earth, as I am frustrated and then willing to submit everything to Him, I will grow into the woman of God I will need to be for the adventure of eternity. That will be handy, just in case eternity is a journey too.

EVERY DAY VINDICATED

A friend commented to me recently that Gabriel visited Zachariah on a normal day. What a silly thought to strike me, and yet it did. Today is a normal day. I do not anticipate all of God's promises to me coming true by noon. Yet, each day is a gift and a continuation of our destiny. Each new day prepares us and moves us closer to the fulfillment of God's promise and purpose for our lives.

It is easy to reason that since we are doing ordinary things, not being married, being married, spending our days wiping noses and fannies, or not spending our days wiping noses and fannies that somehow we are just living in limbo.

In fact it is way too easy to believe that we are living in limbo unless we board a plane on a mission to the nations of the world with the perfect spouse and children by our side, the angels singing, and the heavens rejoicing.

But the reality is that today is the fulfillment of a promise in my life and yours. Wiping fannies, not wiping fannies, married or not, living in your dream house with our without a dream spouse. All are irrelevant. You are part of His plan today.

Big events are big events. They are not the summation of our purpose and destiny. They are just big events. Be patient and let the course of history vindicate the life you lead today. Big or small, every day counts.

DESTINY DETOURS

I find it interesting that when Lewis and Clark made their historic exploration of the North American West they were in their early thirties. And they made history! Yet just a few years afterward, Lewis was so overcome with depression after all the hoopla died down that he took his own life.

How could someone who had achieved so much and still possessed so much potential even consider such a thing?

Yet we all battle that same feeling from time to time. We accomplish something great and then we feel blue after the euphoria of achievement passes. We wallow for a bit and try to decide what to do next. Whether it is coming off a major trip, making a big sale, making it through finals, or whatever it is, the feeling of letdown happens to all of us.

What if we had super hero vision that allowed us to see the traps that the enemy lays for us daily and weekly—detours that lure us from our destiny? These detours are designed to make us think that what we do in the day-to-day is of little to no worth. If we believe that we produce nothing of worth, it is easy to become weary, and the joy we should feel in our own destiny is thwarted.

Investing in people—little children, the elderly—however draining or discouraging it might seem sometimes, has eternal payoffs. Sometimes it is hard to remember that every prayer of every busy person counts, and all our worship, even as we drive down the road, is music to His ears. If we choose to discern the significance of our day-to-day destiny, joy would spill over and out in every direction, running before us and alerting all those we encounter that there is something different coming their way.

Yes, that would be a great goal. Stay on course and spill your destiny on someone today.

TO BE CHILDLIKE

One time when my children were young, a neighbor shot my father's dog. I am sure it was an accident, but it was very upsetting nonetheless. My girls helped nurse the dog all night alongside their grandfather until they fell asleep. During the night the dog finally passed on into doggy heaven.

At breakfast the next morning as we told the girls the terrible news, my oldest, Bethany, began to cry and wail like I have never seen. Allyson quietly got up and walked into her room where she crawled under her bed. My husband, Jeff, Mr. Let-me-pretend I am a child psychiatrist, said, "OK Kath, you stay with Bethany and I will go check on Ally.

Then as I soothingly brushed back the hair of a hysterical four-year-old, he called out, wanting to swap children with me. When I got to the bedroom Allyson was sitting on the side of her bed. She was so small, barely three years old, and she sat on that big bed with her jaw tightly clinched. As I observed my tense looking tot Jeff said, "Now Kath, you take some time to let Allyson share her emotions with you. I will go and comfort Bethany."

I sat down beside my little darling and said, "Honey? How do you feel?'

Meekly and without making eye contact she whispered, "Bad."

I began to assure her that it was good to express herself and encouraged her some more, "how bad sweetheart? Tell me how you feel."

At that moment the proverbial Pandora's Box flew open before me. "I feel BAD," she began to speak louder. Then she repeated it again and again getting louder each time. Then she stood up, threw her arms into the air and railed off every off-limits word she had ever heard.

"I AM SO MAD THAT SOME DUMB, STUUUUUPID, DUH, FAT, PENIS, DUMMY HEAD OF A MAN SHOT MY PAPAW'S DOG!"

Please note that Jeffrey had just been born and the *P* word was totally off limits since the girls were fascinated by the new species that had joined our home. "Head" was a word the kids used in a negative context like saying "silly head." I am not sure to this day how she managed to rattle off something that sounded so sincerely angry with such a limited vocabulary, but she did.

Jeff came running down the hall with a crazed, worried look on his face, asking in his concerned voice, "Honey, what is going on back here?"

"Don't ask the kids to emote if you aren't man enough to take what they spit out." I responded.

I tell you this ridiculous story because sometimes along the journey things happen that neither you nor I can control. Things happen that make me want to stand up and wave my arms around and express my rage against injustice. Sometimes I even wish I could get away with articulating my rage like a three-year-old.

Over the years, we have tried to teach our children what to do with all their emotional energy. Channeled properly, it becomes passion, and passion is the best fuel to fight injustices. Along the journey, there may be a stop or two that all of us must make for justice's sake. Just be ready to let it all out for a good cause.

POLICY VERSUS PRINCIPLE

Policies and procedures will always change. Principles never do. This observation from a friend has resonated with me in light of the state of our homes, our churches, and most of all, our country.

We cannot let our feelings for a policy sway, say, a vote for any elected official. Time has proven that our elected official's policies too often change, leaving us very disappointed. Rather, we must vote on the basis of their principles. If a candidate can, in the face of an emotional policy debate still stand for morality and righteousness then in the end you will not find yourself disappointed.

If we allow policy to triumph over principle, what kind of country do we become? And who is to say that the policy-decision change of the week will be enough to sustain us in a society that already suffers from moral decay.

Policy always changes; principle never does. Be a man or woman of principle in everything you do.

5

Harder Than It Looks

Aging is such a perilous thing. Navigating through life can be treacherous, hard on the ones rowing along with their lives and equally hard on the ones watching from the shore with a different point of view.

My baby boy recently turned thirteen and became a man. During the same month, my daughter turned eighteen and declared herself independent, and my mom turned sixty.

My baby has and always will be my baby. The fact that he now has bushy eyebrows and something fuzzy on his upper lips baffles me. When I close my eyes, he is instantly four again.

Back then he did not want to leave me and go to preschool. We worked on becoming a "big boy" by teaching him to dress himself, brush his own teeth, tie his own shoes, and do all those little things. All so that he could be big and go to preschool. As the day arrived, I waited patiently for him to come down dressed. Finally, I gave in and walked around the corner to find him sitting on the steps in his tighty-whities and undershirt, head in his hands, and a big pouty frown on his face.

"I don't want to grow up and be a big boy. I want to stay a little boy and play with you, Mom. I don't want to be big and go to school."

I open my eyes again and he is tall. He stands so tall that my memories are challenged. He still does not want to go to school, but that no longer has anything to do with me. Little Jeffy has a sense of who he is becoming, and he is trying his best to figure out how to get there.

Bethany Anne, my firstborn, is a work of art. She is complex and beautiful and much time has gone into her becoming a young woman. Again, I feel the need to close my eyes and live in the past. She was so cute with her fluffy cheeks singing, "Skinamarinky dinky doo. I love you."

I sang to her every day when she was little, and she sang back to me endlessly. She told me one day that no one in her life can just lay everything out for her and put her on a path. It is her path, and she must discover it on her own to grow in her own strength.

Can there be anything more painful for an artist than when her artwork gets ready to leave the studio? I know she has strength, but I am not sure I am strong enough to allow her to find it. Over the years we have had to come to terms over things like tattoos and nose piercing, and yet it seems so surreal that I even have to have these conversations. I was not ready. I do not feel done with this masterpiece yet.

My mother, Martha, has been and always shall be the most beautiful woman to grace this earth. She is a lady in every sense of the word. Even her name means lady. She wears elegance, graciousness, hospitality, and love like a supermodel wears couture. I close my eyes, and she is a Natalie Wood look-alike, and we traipse around the country because Dad is in the military.

Never has anyone traipsed in such a lovely manner. I wonder if I will age as well, if I will be so well thought of, and if I will be so gracious.

She has taught me how to adore my future grandchildren and how to make my own children a priority. I love that about her. As we celebrated her sixtieth birthday, I wondered if she still feels anxious watching me navigate my own way into the river of womanhood. She has handled it better than I have, I am certain of that.

Life is a journey that demands that our passports be stamped periodically as we enter into a new country. We must travel. Some moments, I want nothing more than to stop it all and just sit and have homemade hot chocolate with my babies again. I understand that I myself am rowing and navigating; yet I am standing still watching time pass and my treasures grow.

Maybe it is the releasing that launches my own boat into new, unseen adventures. I do not want to miss celebrating major milestones because I have closed my eyes. I do not want to miss the boat.

Aging is definitely harder than it looks.

BAD FOOD AND BINGO

As my grandmother, Kathryn, got up there in years, we realized that aging was not an easy process for her. We did not realize until some time later that she had Alzheimer's. As she gradually found it harder to do for herself, we found a wonderful assisted living center near our homes and helped her get settled in to her new place.

On the first full day she was there I stopped by around dinnertime to find her sitting with pursed lips and a scowl that would scare small children. I sat down beside her and asked what was wrong.

"Do you see this?" she asked, showing me what appeared to be a very nice meal of meat and vegetables. "They call this dinner!"

"It looks good to me," I encouraged.

Obviously, we disagreed. Finally, the server came back around and offered my grandmother a large piece of chocolate pie. She nodded, but would not look the server in the eye as if she were still pouting. She reached out her fork, but before she could snatch a bite, I pulled the pie away and got a fork for myself.

"What do you think you are doing?" she asked.

"You can't have dessert until you have dinner. Take a bite of dinner and I will let you have a bite of pie." I said.

I know that sounded mean even though I was grinning, but sometimes you just have to be firm. She squinted her eyes and stared me down. I smiled back. She took her fork and tasted her roast beef. Then I let her take a very large bite of pie. This went on until both plates were clean and all the while she complained about the bad food.

I knew the food was not really bad. I tasted it. I thought it was actually pretty good. It was nothing like her homemade cooking, but it was good in a cafeteria sort of way.

Eventually Granny Kat settled into a happy routine. She made friends, ate the food (notice I did not say enjoyed) and seemed glad to be alive. One day I came to visit with a bag of M&Ms in hand and noticed a half-dozen stuffed animals all over her room. This was not her style, and it was extremely odd to see stuffed toys sitting on her priceless antiques.

"Granny Kat, where did all this come from?" I asked.

"B-I-N-G-O!" she exclaimed joyously. "I won it all playing bingo."

I drove home that day, confused. I wondered if this is what life is all about: bad food and bingo. *Is this what we have to look forward to?* I wondered.

Not long after that, my parents were out of town so I got the late night call from the assisted living home. The nurse pleaded with me to come quickly and told me my grandmother was in a terrible state. I went immediately, and what I found changed everything. I could hear her yelling as I entered the front door.

My beautiful grandmother who was the best cook and seamstress in town had a nightgown on backwards and her hair was all disheveled in a crazy and wild way. There were aids clamoring all around her trying to get her to calm down. I asked them to leave, and without thought, I calmed her and scooped up her frail body, which had always been so voluptuous, and laid her in her bed.

I climbed up beside her as she shook violently, asking me who I was and what I was doing there. She wanted her son, my dad, and he was not answering his phone, which upset her. She was calling a phone number from thirty years before. I wanted to protect her; I wanted to protect myself. I wanted more for her than this.

I pulled myself up in the bed closer beside her and could feel the Father's love from heaven over her. I felt a strange calmness that only God can provide and I began to tell her a story about a grand lady named Kathryn. She calmed down and eventually laid her head on my shoulder as I recounted her tales that she had often told me of her days as a young girl in Alabama.

I told her of her wedding and honeymoon, her children, her mother, and even her love for cooking. I told her the whole story about a lady named Kathryn while I played with her soft white hair.

When I was done, she said, "That lady was something else. Did you know her personally or did someone just tell you this story?"

As I cried, still holding her, I told her I had the supreme privilege of knowing her well.

When her time came to pass on to heaven she had not spoken in some weeks, but just before the end she rallied and was briefly semi aware. My father and mother and husband and I were there with her as I slid in to the bed beside her once more.

"Granny Kat, I am here. This is Kathy, your namesake, and I just want you to know that I love you."

She groaned back a rusty sounding, "I love you too." Needless to say, we all wept.

At her funeral, I shared this story and told everyone there that when you hold the hand of someone you love in the last season of his or her life, you have a responsibility to learn something. That is the purpose; it's not just bad food and bingo.

God allows us to share the road with others so that we may receive and so that we may give. So often we think that we are doing all the giving only to realize we are the ones left with a treasure box. The greatest gift my grandmother, Kathryn, ever gave me was the revelation that even though the mind forgets, the heart never does.

We must love with our hearts.

SEASONS OF BEAUTY

I am blessed with teenage daughters—three, to be exact—and one son, rounding out the group to make an even four. On any given day at any given moment, one of them has an opinion about me. Most of the time that is fine with me, but there are days when I wonder if I will make it and live to tell the story or raising four children into wonderful, productive adults.

The mothering epiphany hit me one day as I felt my knees buckle under the weighty judgments of a fourteen-year-old who knew everything. Thankfully it hit me; she is exactly like me.

As a matter of fact she will one day be middle-aged, and she will one day walk in similar shoes. One day her face creams will outnumber her hair products, and we will be equal. This revelation empowered me.

If I, being a wise woman, bend into a teenager's view of me, who would be leading who? If I, however, embrace who I am in all my quirkiness at all stages of life, then I show my daughters the platform of confidence from which they too can launch themselves into the wide world.

Beauty is found within. Not in a pair of jeans, a style of clothing, or a new haircut (although a good haircut never hurt anyone), but true beauty is only found within.

I have been twenty, I did that already, and I do not have to do it again. I have been thirty-something as well; it was a fun ride, but now there is another one waiting. If I spend this season allowing opinionated children to make me relive my own teen years for the sake of coolness or popular opinion, then I do nothing but rob them of their own chance to mature into the beautiful women I already know they are.

Every season of life is to be embraced, and in every stage of a woman's life, beauty can be found beneath the surface. No chemical peel necessary.

LIFE IS A GIFT

Talking with a cancer survivor always brings perspective into our lives. Recently, I encountered a woman who I expected to share that predictable story. Predictable in the sense that I knew she would tell me how her life is a gift and how she had learned how to appreciate it. I have heard and learned from many people in that state of life, so I thought I knew what to expect.

What caught me off guard was the story she told me of her neighbor's life, not her own. She told me of an elderly woman who had lived next door to her for years. When the cancer survivor was going through chemotherapy, the decrepit, old woman would come over to help her out the best that she could, which usually consisted of fetching a glass of water or handing her medication.

One day as they conversed, the cancer survivor noted the age and seeming strain in her neighbor's face and asked how she was doing.

"I am acquainted with the sufferings of Christ, my dear, and that is a blessing." Not long after that, the elderly woman passed away.

The cancer survivor teared up as she shared her epiphany with me that our journeys are to be shared. If life is a gift, then we should give it. Our journey is not our own; we are meant to encourage, strengthen, and even cheer on those we are leaving behind.

We may be on a pilgrimage to eternity, but while we are traveling, we have to ask ourselves if we accept each day as a gift to bless others with. Some of those days are good and easy, and some are not. My journey is not my own. Neither is yours.

WE ARE BUT VAPORS

Our life is just a vapor. If we are but a vapor then what exactly does that mean? Isn't it like the visible vapor what we see when we exhale in the winter months? We see our breath? I suppose it is an interaction of elements that causes the invisible to come together and become visible, if only fleetingly.

What if God, the breather of life, is breathing right now through us? Wouldn't it cause all creation to see, the visible effect of His breath meeting the cold world and resulting in our lives: a vapor.

However brief our stay is here, it is only His exhaling that gives us life and his DNA that gives us image. We are but a vapor. But a vapor with a purpose! Selah.

The good news is that God is patient with slow-learners and that is why he shares epiphanies with us, sometimes more than once. We can try as hard as we like, but even on our best days, we are far too insignificant to conquer the challenges that face us in this life.

Some days the road is easy, and the sun is shining, our children obey, and we have extra to share. Some days are hard, perilous even, and the suffering can suffocate us. It is in both times that we must remain faithful in our journey to rely totally on the compass from Him.

6

VEERING OFF

"**Ouch, stop it,** you're hurting me!" we cry to our moms as they braid our hair.

In my case, all Mom had to do to earn a squeal was try to brush out the tangles from the curly, brown bush that grew from my head. As we later learn, this is really just a little, and necessary, discomfort. But to the young, the pain is all too real.

We have all experienced pain in our adult lives too. If you have not, please come talk to me; I want your recipe.

I do not like pain. I have never been a fan of pain and do not even see the point. But pain happens, just like getting lost on a back road. Years ago, my husband and I started a new church, yet after we were several years into it, we were a shredded mess.

Have you ever been a part of starting a church in a new city? Call me, and we can start a support group. Suffice it to say that I had detoured off the course that I needed to be on, plain and simple. I didn't mean to; there was no conscious choice, no examination of a map and a decision, "Hey, I think I will take this side road and hope I get where I am supposed to be going."

It was more like I lost focused on the road for one moment and found myself veering off course. The road ran parallel long enough to deceive me, and then suddenly I was miles off base. Darn, I hate that.

During that season, life just seemed hard. Everything seemed hard. I felt hard. There was a wonderful young woman that I had been somewhat of a mentor to who bravely came up to me one day and said, "Kathy, I love you, but you have fallow ground and it needs to be plowed."

Now there is a bold statement! I looked at her and even though everything in me wanted to say it was not so, it was so. I had veered. Sometimes epiphanies don't come from within; they come from the outside, and those seem to hurt more. But, like your mom brushing or braiding your hair, we have to look at the intent. My friend's heart was pure, and she was right. Darn, I hate that too.

I had a choice (there are those choices again). I could have defended myself and explained how simple my mistake was and how getting off course was an accident. I could have been indignant and told her that when she was my age and had experienced life, then and only then could she speak into my life. I could have said all kinds of things. I thought of them all that day, and for some days after, to be honest.

But the word of God says that God resists the proud and gives grace to the humble, and so I thought since I obviously needed some grace I decided I had better go low. I remember looking at her young face and humbly repenting for my error.

The harder part was allowing someone younger to walk shoulder to shoulder with me after that. There was equality in someone my age, and authority in someone older, but no one my age or older spoke into my life that day. Instead it was a young twenty-something. She was gracious, I was willing to take another look at the map before me, and together we got things back on course.

The truth is, the excuses I wanted to offer that day would have done nothing but hurt me, my family, and my church, but the path I chose instead did wonders to help. The truth is fallow ground happens, hard things happen, hardness happens and so does veering. Interestingly, when we begin to walk in humility, God's grace greets us, and we get back on course. It was not painless, but the way I figure it, neither was the cross, and in light of that, I always get off easy.

JUST AS I WAS FORGIVEN, LET ME FORGIVE

Forgiveness and unforgiveness are funny things. They are funny because they have layers, like an onion. Some days the stench fills your life. Mine anyway. Several years ago when I was in the midst of a battle of forgiveness, I wrote down these thoughts as I pressed into a deeper place and studied the relationship Jesus shared with Judas.

A Kiss

What did it feel like when he kissed you, my Lord? Was it a tangible revelation of what the Father had already revealed? Did your heart weep, or did you hold out hope?

When you cried out in the garden, did you see his face? When you closed your eyes? When the Father told you of your mission, did he send the Holy Spirit with His kisses? Did the pain remain?

When you saw him coming, was your heart tender? Did you wish and pray that your heart could harden? If you had not given him your heart, would it have hurt? Was there ever a choice? Was your heart pure when you called him friend? Was it enough to give that gift without having it returned? What did it feel like? Did your Father's kisses hold you?

When he leaned in, did you look into his eyes? Did he look into yours? Was the smell of his embrace familiar to you and strangely comforting? When his lips met your cheek, what did it feel like?

Did the kiss linger? As you were taken? As you were beaten and stripped? Did you cry out for your friend? Did your face sting as tears fell across the same place once endeared? When you were on the cross did you cry out for mercy for him? When you could no longer feel your Father's kisses, did you remember his? Did you still call him friend? What did it feel like?

Oh, but then. When your Father held you, did he kiss you on the forehead? Did he cover your whole face as he pronounced, "Well done"? Is His embrace eternal? What does it feel like?

I thought of this poem when I went back to the city where I once lived and where my husband ministered at a church more than a decade previously. I saw people that had hurt one another years earlier. It was odd and yet amazing to watch them ministering together in unity once again.

Then a few days later I talked to a friend who was suffering. My heart broke over and over at the thought of the betrayal she was going through. As I drove home, I passed an old friend who no longer wanted to relate with us. I remembered one of our last conversations in which I lightly said, "Well, you know, more faithful is the wound of a friend than the kiss of an enemy."

He dropped his head and smiled and said, "Yeah, but the kiss sure feels good."

Would I give up one minute with these old friends for an inch I have grown deeper in the Lord? Absolutely not.

I would have gained no inkling of understanding of what the depths of eternity look like had it not been for the pain of betrayal. Those terrible moments also remain a constant reminder of why my gaze is fixed on eternity.

Some things are not or cannot be resolved here. Some things are meant to grow us and teach us and stir up something in us to dive deeper for the more, for His view rather than ours, for His kiss rather than a friend's. Painful as it can be, better is one day in His court than a thousand elsewhere.

Forgiveness is a funny thing. The deeper you go with the Father, the higher the view He shares with you. I'll take that any day.

IT ALL WORKS OUT IN THE END, SO IF IT HASN'T WORKED OUT, IT'S NOT THE END

As we journey through life, it is easy to praise God when things are going along nicely, but when things are not running smoothly, the praise on our lips becomes the very life preserver we need.

I look back to when my children were small, and I can measure the growth in my strength and ability to endure by the seasons I lived through. I have learned many important things, and each one taught me something about who I am and who I am called to be. Those lessons taught me who I was raising from His view, not my own.

But what if I had gotten what I wished for and had been spared financial hardship, or deprivation of quality time when I wanted it, or sleep—precious, precious sleep. What if?

It was in hardship, that I saw the Father's provision in those seasons of abundant mercy and grace. It was divine. Because of loneliness, I learned to press on through, by praising Him. And, it was in the night, that God shared his secrets with me about my children. It was the foundation of my revelation that He has called me to be a watchman. I would have missed that revelation if I had children who would sleep.

I do not want to go back in time and repeat any of it, thank you very much, but I count it all joy that I was able to posture myself to receive His mercy. If we do not posture ourselves through a heart of gratitude and praise to receive the good He has for us, we will never come to the end of anything; we will just perpetuate the season of learning.

I know that there is so much more that the Father has for me as a woman, wife, mother, and Pastor's wife. I have prayed for years for "the more" from God. Good, bad and other, I want the more. If it is His more, then I want it. I know we can trust Him to give us perfect gifts that are for our benefit. He is faithful and if something has not worked out for you yet in any area of your life, then I encourage you to press into Him and receive the good gifts and lessons He has chosen to strengthen you for the journey ahead.

SHIFT HAPPENS

While having lunch one day with a dear friend, she opened my eyes to a harsh reality in life. We were discussing our ever-changing seasons as women, as mother's, and as wives.

That is when she broke it to me, "Kath, you can read *Who Moved My Cheese?* all day long, but the bottom line is, shift happens. Deal with it."

Isn't it wonderful to have friends who will just slap you in the face with the truth when you need it?

PILLOW TALK

Years ago, I turned thirty. I couldn't wait. I think it was because I am short.

You understand don't you? Short people are often overlooked, are not heard, and can never reach things on the top shelf of life. I had this fantasy that once I reached thirty I would suddenly have more stature by life's measuring stick.

I told my friends as I traveled through my twenties that I knew I would finally have arrived once I turned thirty. Of course, the day came and went, and at thirty years and one day, I woke up the same height as the day before. I was a little disappointed.

But a dear friend called and asked me to join her for lunch so that she could share her gift with me. Being a plan-ahead kind of person, she had ordered it from a catalog five months before the big day. After all my hype and hopes for thirty, she wanted to bless me with a memorable gift for that special birthday.

Her gift became a life lesson, an epiphany that steers me even today.

As we sat down in our favorite eatery she placed a large yellow gift bag on the table. First things first, of course the gift had to be opened. I noticed that there were several gifts in the bag, and she told me this story as I opened them.

"About five months ago, I ordered you a lovely pillow for your room that would say, 'QUEEN KATHRYN' in the perfect blue to match your room. About six weeks later, I came home and found a box on my doorstep. I opened it excitedly only to find a lovely red pillow that proclaimed brightly, 'KING KATHRYN.'"

"I thought it was funny and knew that I had plenty of time to return it, so I called the company. Now the company explained that this kind of thing never happened and that they would put a new pillow in the mail right away."

At this point, she allowed me to open the first gift to find the KING KATHRYN pillow. I laughed.

"Then about three or four weeks passed, and I came home from work to find another box on my porch. I knew it must surely be your pillow. So I ripped open the box only to find, not a pillow, but a cover for the pillow. This cover was also red instead of blue and the front proudly proclaimed, 'KING QUEEN KATHRYN.'"

I laughed again as she let me open the next gift. I must say that I was wondering who embroideries these things.

She continued, "Then I called the company who explained that this kind of thing *never* happens and that they would send me out a correct pillow right away.

I told them that this was crazy and that I certainly expect them to do so as it was getting dangerously close to your actual birthday."

"About three or four weeks later," she continued, "I came home from work to find another box on my porch. Now you can imagine that at this point, I was a little skeptical, especially as I got closer to the box. It wasn't even the same size as the other boxes. And when I picked it up it made a clunking noise!"

She pushed the bag across the table to me. I was shocked at the heaviness of the box and you can easily imagine my surprise after all the pillow talk, when I opened the package to find a silver-plated wine cooler with the name "MCFAD-DEN" engraved on it.

I laughed pretty loudly at this point. She continued with the story, laughing herself, "Well, you know I called the company who told me that this *NEEEEEVER* happens, and I just interrupted them and said, 'well, YEEEEEES it does! Because I have had three mess-ups when all I wanted was a blue Queen Kathryn pillow for my friend who is turning thirty, and that should not have been too much to ask from a company that sells them.' The lady on the phone calmed me down and promised that a pillow would be sent right out.

"Just a few days ago, I came home to find a small box waiting on the porch. Nervously, I opened the box to find …"

She gestured towards the bag again. I was delighted to find a lovely blue pillow that proudly proclaimed me, "Queen Kathryn." I smiled and said, "Ah, this is lovely. Thank you so much!" But, as I picked up the pillow and held it close to my heart, I felt something flap behind my hand. Turning the pillow over, I discovered the horror that the back of the pillow was ripped all along the corner.

Confused, I looked at my friend, who continued, "Ah, yes. That was my reaction exactly. I showed my husband when he got home. He thought I would be tempting fate to call the company again and suggested that I simply sew up the torn corner. But you know what, it came down to principle. So I called the company anyway.

"Just as the little voice at the other end began to say this 'never happens,' I yelled into the phone, 'you listen to me, lady, this does happen. It happens all the time … TO ME!'

"'I want a Queen Kathryn pillow, and if I don't have it in the right color with the right words within twenty-four hours, I will fly to California personally to deal with you and your customer service team!'"

With that off her chest, my friend explained the whole saga to the customer service representative who was extremely apologetic, especially over the McFadden's wine cooler.

"Finally, yesterday on your birthday, I came home to find another box on the porch. Cautiously, I opened it and inside was a perfectly perfect blue pillow that said, 'QUEEN KATHRYN'.'" She let me reach into the bag for the final gift. I opened it up and held that perfect pillow close.

Life is a lot like that gift. We think we have planned accordingly. We have mapped out our way and have plenty of time to spare. We think the choices we have made will get us to our chosen destination. Only life has unexpected turns in the road, and we find ourselves off course.

We pray and we wonder if God is hearing us (KING KATHRYN). We keep on going, staying the course, and life's highway has a dip and a bend, and again we find ourselves asking God for direction. Alas, all we seem to get is more questions (KING QUEEN KATHRYN).

We have a choice here. Some stop. They pull over to the side of the road and break down. Don't. Don't pull over. Don't stop. Keep going.

Keep going even when you wonder if God even knows your name (McFadden's wine cooler). The truth is He does. He has plans for you, and they are plans for you to prosper. Keep going.

When the bumps in the road come out of nowhere and you hit them too fast, when you think you are going to wreck, break down or feel lost … keep going. When you drive up to a place that looks almost as good as your destination and you feel tempted to settle … don't (torn pillow). Don't settle. Don't strive to figure out a way to make it work. Press on.

When we stay the course and press on we get the prize. 1 Corinthians 9:24 says, "I run that I may win, not the intangible crown but the tangible" (NIV).

Run that you may win. Trust HIM and He will take you on the ride of your life.

The journey continues. Each day we wake up, we find ourselves greeted with a myriad of opportunities for new adventures and new choices. That is possibly the greatest epiphany so far, the part of the map that has yet to be revealed. I am more confident today than I was yesterday that we can trust epiphanies to guide us along life's way.

Every woman has a journey to travel. No two paths are exactly the same, no two roads are alike, and yet the maps are all strikingly similar. Each map tells us to relax and follow the road before us, trust ourselves, pit stops are OK as long as we don't stay too long, detours happen, fuel is necessary, always keep our identification and our minds with us at all times, take pictures along the way, and, most important, stay the course.

THANKS

Pastor Beth Moore teaches that everyone should have "stretcher bearers" in their lives—people who love you enough to carry you to Jesus when you really need it; people who love you unconditionally "in spite of."

I am so blessed to have friends and family that would do just that for me. My husband Jeff is the greatest. Thank you for your support and your coaching me through the last twenty-plus years. I could not have made this journey without you, and I would not have wanted to. Every year I am married to you, I love you more than the year before. Thank you, Jesus! To my children, the greatest treasures I have been given, I dedicate this book and all the other daily wisdom that I will continue to throw at you. Thank you for enduring my endless stories.

To my family, the nucleus of love, my parents, Hal and Marty Glasgow, my brother, David Glasgow, my sister, Mary Ellen Smith, and her hubby, Tim, and my grandmother, Granny Ree, thank you for showing me your support with action. Thank you for forcing me to sit down and write this book. Thank you for your love and all the wonderful memories we have shared over our lives that have helped enlighten me. You have blessed me more than I deserve and enriched me beyond worth. You have helped shape and define me and have given me strength and heritage to discover who I am in God.

To my extended family, I want to say that you all have been such an inspiration for me. Lord knows you have not only experienced the epiphanies with me but have had to listen to me tell you over and over the newest and latest. Sam and Sammye Oakes, Lynn and Lora Dowling, Betty and Darin Hale, and all the rest of our great big clan, thank you.

My stretcher bearers are my Valley Girlfriends. Thank you Angie, Jacque, Kim, Cindy, Ellen, Karen, and our "little sisters" Julie, Brandy, Bethany P, Beckah, and Betsy, you all keep me going. I am so blessed to have all of you in my life. Each of you is an irreplaceable treasure.

Thanks to the Gracious-Heads, you know who you are, for listening and laughing on so many Saturdays at my mother's store while this book was being written. And to all of the blog readers who have sent words of encouragement from all over the world.

A special thanks to my friend, Jim Greer, for making Jeff and I laugh for twenty-plus years, for marrying us, and for remaining our lifelong friend. Thank you, Matthew Wine, for your faithfulness and for showing me what a brother in the Lord looks like. I have learned so much from you both.

Most importantly, I would like to thank God for His enduring love for me and all humanity. He loves us all so much that He was willing to sacrifice His only Son for us. We are not worthy, and yet we are redeemed and loved. Thank you, Father, for not giving me what I deserve and in its stead granting me freedom in you. Thank you for allowing me to wake up breathing every day. In my quest and in my journey, thank you for showing me your beauty in day-to-day life and in creation.

About the Author

Mother, wife, sister, daughter, writer, working girl, photographer, storyteller and princess, Kathy Oakes finally, and with great fanfare, crossed the line to join millions of women doing just fine after forty.

She lives quite comfortably in Johnson City, Tennessee, with her husband, Jeff, who is a pastor, three clever, beautiful daughters, and a talented and handsome son who all provide much of the inspiration, or at least impetus, for her epiphanies.

978-0-595-48125-5
0-595-48125-6